UNKNOWN TO UNSTOPPABLE

A Commercial Real Estate Broker's Guide to Dominating Your Market

NATHAN MATELICH, CCIM

PEAK REAL ESTATE SERVICES

Unknown to Unstoppable: A Commercial Real Estate Broker's Guide to Dominating Your Market
Published by Peak Real Estate Services LLC
Billings, Montana, U.S.A.

MATELICH, NATHAN, Author
UNKNOWN TO UNSTOPPABLE
NATHAN MATELICH

Library of Congress Control Number: 2022923215

ISBN: 979-8-9873381-0-0, 979-8-9873381-1-7 (paperback)
ISBN: 979-8-9873381-2-4 (hardcover)
ISBN: 979-8-9873381-3-1 (digital)

BUSINESS & ECONOMICS / Real Estate / Commercial
BUSINESS & ECONOMICS / Leadership
BUSINESS & ECONOMICS / Personal Success

Publishing Team: Rogue Publishing Partners (roguepublishingpartners.com)
Editing: Scott Sery (scottsery.com)
Editing: Jennifer Jas (wordswithjas.com)
Book Design: Michelle M. White (mmwbooks.com)
Publishing Management: Susie Schaefer (finishthebookpublishing.com)

QUANTITY PURCHASES:
Schools, companies, professional groups, clubs, and other organizations
may qualify for special terms when ordering quantities of this title.
For information, email nathan@cbcmontana.com.

This book is printed in the United States of America.

This book is dedicated to all those
who have helped me on the path to success:

My wife, Heidi Matelich, and our five amazing kids.
My mom and dad, Craig and Mary Matelich.
My mentors Steve Kenney, George Warmer,
Blaine Poppler, and David Mitchell.
My assistant, Cindy Tapp.

CONTENTS

INTRODUCTION TO MARKET DOMINATION

I will be honest. This isn't your typical real estate book. In fact, I don't even like calling it a book. Think of this more as a commercial real estate broker's *guide* to market domination. This short, revolutionary guide is the product of a seven-year-long quest to go from a brand-new commercial real estate broker in a city where I didn't know anyone to the **#1 producing commercial real estate broker in the state of Montana**.

With sales surpassing $50 million, I earned the Platinum Circle of Distinction at Coldwell Banker Commercial, the highest award and one that is typically only seen by brokers in large metros like Chicago, New York City, or Los Angeles. I used the trade secrets outlined in this guide to sell so much real estate in my first two years that my partners had no choice but to invite me to join them as a Broker/Owner of Coldwell Banker Commercial CBS. Within four years, I consistently had 40 to 50 listings, making me the top listing broker in Billings, Montana. I don't share these stats to brag but to show you that if I can achieve this level of success in a tertiary market where I had no prior real estate experience or connections, then you *absolutely* can too.

This publication is more of a guide than a book because I wanted to put together a step-by-step playbook that *any* new real estate broker could read in less than an hour and have easy-to-implement action steps that will at least double the size of their current real estate business. Over the last four years, I have been responsible for recruiting, training, and mentoring new brokers at Coldwell Banker Commercial CBS. This guide is the finished product of what I've used to train all our new brokers, who have gone on to sell ***double and triple*** the amount of real estate I sold during my first year in the business.

While some of these real estate tools and tactics aren't new, I can say with certainty that this is the first time these "trade secrets" and the "secret sauce" have been compiled together in a straight-to-the-point guide that guarantees stratospheric success without having to read a boring 250-page book. Keep reading if you want to:

- Dominate your real estate market
- Become the #1 most-referred realtor
- Consistently have 40 to 50 listings
- Double your income in the next 6 to 12 months
- Achieve top producer status in your company

I'll see you at the top ... because the bottom is already full!

UNPACKING SUCCESS

A decade and a half ago, I was living in Chicago while attending school for an MBA in finance. I knew little about real estate, but I saw a good deal for a duplex hit the market. Immediately, I recalled the Warren Buffett quote that advises us to be "fearful when others are greedy, and greedy when others are fearful."

Everyone needs a place to live, so I pulled together the last of my student loans to use as a down payment. I rounded up a couple of friends, and we lived in one-half of the duplex while renting the other half out. With rent from the roommates and tenants, I brought in more than 100% of the cost of living there.

Shortly after I moved in, my friend Matthew Hernandez visited. When he saw how I had structured the deal, he looked me in the eye and said, "Nate, you real estate mogul, you."

I laughed it off. I wasn't in real estate; I was a poor grad student just barely scraping by. But I did know a good deal when I saw one. This became my introduction to real estate.

In 2008, as the financial crisis came crashing down around the country, I was laid off from my job. I thought my only source of income had dried up, but I soon realized I actually had an income stream from my duplex: a safety net that many of my friends couldn't fall back on. I became obsessed with creating these multiple streams of residual income.

As I sat on my couch, unemployed but living for free, it was time for a big decision. If I was going to become self-employed and pursue a career as an entrepreneur, I had to first learn how to become an expert marketer before I could sell anything for my own business.

So I read every business, marketing, and entrepreneur book I could find. I took notes, underlined, and employed the tactics I learned. I became a marketer first, above all else.

I met my wife in Chicago. She had grown up in Billings, and we decided it was time to head back to Montana. We sold the duplex and had a healthy capital gain on that property. With mounds of student debt, I had to make a choice: pay off those loans or keep pursuing that "real estate mogul" status.

We decided to invest in a triplex. We rented the other two units to pay for the entire mortgage. I knew that real estate was the route I wanted to take; now I had to decide what kind of realtor I planned to be.

Real estate falls into two categories: residential and commercial. With one of my core values being spending quality time with my family, residential real estate didn't seem like a good fit. Many transactions are done after hours and on the weekends.

So, commercial it was.

As with many sales positions, selling real estate involves building relationships. When I moved to Billings, it took only one hand to count the number of people I knew. That meant I had to figure out something fast, or I would never make it in this market.

That's why I developed the new school approach to marketing real estate. It wasn't enough to put up a sign, throw the listing on my website, and cross my fingers. Instead, I pulled out that old journal, reviewed the time-tested concepts I had learned, and created a new process to apply them to commercial real estate and skyrocket my success.

Every time a client trusted me to list their property, I went through a 30- to 40-point checklist (see "Time-saving Tasks for

Your Assistant" starting on page 99) to ensure it was listed properly and would get in front of the people who would ultimately be in the market for that property.

During my first year at Coldwell Banker Commercial, I earned $40,000. That wasn't too bad; it was pretty average for those first entering this profession. The following year, however, I ramped it up and more than doubled my income.

My success was so quick that I made partner in the brokerage by the end of my second year. Looking back, I suppose it was a way to ensure I stuck around and didn't start my own brokerage, but it sparked something in me. It meant that I had the responsibility to not only grow my business but to guide every broker in the building to their success as well.

Over the years, I have consistently maintained 40 to 50 listings under my name. In this industry, a successful broker usually maintains 10 to 15 listings. Those 40 listings in four years became the inspiration for this book.

This book isn't a humblebrag about my success. It delivers the action-packed steps so you can do what I did and launch yourself to success but do it faster.

I'm not working for just me anymore. I'm working for every broker I mentor. I have this system down, and I'm constantly perfecting it, so I know my success will always be there.

Now, I'm working with you. I'm mentoring you along the way so your first year isn't a mere $40,000 but double – or triple – that amount. I know it's possible because I've seen it happen repeatedly in our Billings office.

But now it's time for a decision: Are you ready to become unstoppable?

PART I

HIGH-PERFORMANCE MINDSET

1

LEADERS ARE READERS

If you want to achieve Level 10 success in your real estate career, you *must* first develop yourself into a Level 10 person.

For most of my life, I did not like reading. As I worked on my MBA, I discovered business, personal development, and other self-help books. I realized there were great books that I could immediately turn around and apply the concepts to my life.

Quickly, I went from reading half a book per year to 50+ books per year, simply because I discovered that a CEO reads an average of 60 books in any given year.

I applied those concepts and extracted the best ones to share here. I highly recommend that after reading this guide, start working your way through the books on the Recommended Reading List (see page 95) and add your own ideas to the list.

To be at the top, you must devote yourself to pursuing knowledge nonstop.

ACTION STEP

Create a part of your routine that involves reading at least 10 pages per day so you are continually growing and learning.

2

CREATE A MORNING ROUTINE

Read *The Miracle Morning* or *The Miracle Morning for Real Estate Agents*, both by Hal Elrod. These books will change your life.

When I lived in Chicago, I experienced a moderate amount of success. I had an average job that provided me with an average income. My life was filled with mediocrity, and I experienced a passable amount of happiness.

I read the book *The Miracle Morning* and realized that the piece of the equation that would allow me to springboard off that "average" plateau was to fine-tune my morning routine.

You can do this in six steps:

1. **Write down your goals** and review them every day. Stay firm in your goals but flexible in your path. Use a vision board, a journal, or even an app on your phone to keep those goals focused.
2. **Exercise**. Training your body increases productivity dramatically.
3. **Read** at least 10 pages per day.
4. **Visualize your ideal real estate career** and reverse engineer it. Break it down into daily, weekly, and monthly tasks.
5. **Journal**. Write down five things you are thankful for every day. Plan your day by listing the three to five tasks you must accomplish. Consider getting The Five Minute Journal or The High Performance Journal.

6. **Pray, meditate, or simply enjoy the silence** of the morning. Prepare mentally for the day. You can attack the day, or it can attack you – your choice.

ACTION STEP

Create a schedule including these actions and follow it *without exception* every day for at least 21 days so these actions become habits.

3
KILLER PRODUCTIVITY

"If it's your job to eat a frog, it's best to do it first thing in the morning. And if it's your job to eat two frogs, it's best to eat the biggest one first." - Mark Twain

I'm not in the habit of eating frogs, but Mark Twain's comment is about getting the biggest, hardest, or worst things done right away so you can sail through the rest of your day.

The secret to avoiding killed productivity and achieving killer productivity is to time block your day and tackle the most important work first. Then, you can be satisfied with the day as you get things done before the phone starts ringing and kills your productivity.

I maintain a written list of every single task I must get done. Some need to be done today, tomorrow, next week, next month, or even next year.

At the end of each day, I review my list and write down the top three to five tasks that must be done the following day to feel like it will be successful.

Does this always work?

Yes, it does ... unless you don't put in the work.

The times I have failed are the times when I get lazy. The days when I stay up too late, sleep through my miracle morning, and start the day off grumpy and without enough rest or coffee – those days turn into a train wreck. I have five children under 10 years old. If I don't get my miracle morning done before they start their day, I am not giving them the time they deserve before the phone starts ringing.

You either own and conquer the day, or the day owns and conquers you.

ACTION STEP

1. **Time block your most important work. I often do it at 6 or 7 a.m. to ensure I start the day off right.**
2. **Eat your big frog first. Do the most difficult, important tasks first thing in the morning while you have energy and focus.**
3. **Tackle the tough conversations that move deals forward. They should be your first calls of the day.**

4

HAVE A LIFE OUTSIDE OF REAL ESTATE

I chose commercial real estate because it allowed me the flexibility of having evenings and weekends off. That means I work incredibly hard Monday through Friday from 8 a.m. to 5 or 6 p.m. When it's time to quit for the day, I recharge my mind outside of work.

Many psychological studies have shown that when you hit 50 hours in your work week, productivity drops so dramatically that continuing to work is a waste of time.

When 5 or 5:30 p.m. rolls around, I jot a quick note about what I need to do the next day, and I leave work at work. Going home to my family – without the stress of work hanging over my head – means I can focus on them. We spend our weekends camping, fishing, skiing, or simply enjoying the things we love because work tasks get done at work.

When it's time to return to the office, my body and mind are recharged. I'm ready to take on the world because I haven't drained myself by overworking.

Top-producing commercial real estate brokers avoid working on the weekends like the plague so they can rest, relax, and recharge. Enjoy interesting hobbies for yourself; they might also become your best conversation pieces with clients.

ACTION STEP

We all have hobbies. List your top three to five hobbies, and structure your off time so you can enjoy them.

5

LEARN FROM OTHERS WHO ARE MORE SUCCESSFUL THAN YOU

I credit a large part of my success to the mentors I had for the first year of my commercial real estate career.

When meeting people, networking, and finding potential prospects, I wouldn't know what the opportunities were, but I gathered the information and brought it back to Steve Kenney, my mentor. He would train me and help me serve those clients while I was still learning how to spot incredible opportunities.

It goes deeper than just asking for advice. Take your mentors out to lunch. Ask them how they grew their business, and take excellent notes. You don't need an original idea to be successful; you just need to find the most successful person in your field and imitate what they do while putting your own spin on it to remain authentic.

Here are six great questions that John Maxwell suggests we ask our mentors:

1. What is the greatest lesson you have learned?
2. What are you learning now?
3. How has failure shaped your life?
4. Who do you know whom I should know?
5. What have you done that I should do?
6. How can I add value to you?

Make a habit of taking the top brokers in your office out to lunch and asking them what their key to success is. Shadow top brokers for a day. Figure out how to systematically work it into your daily routine via your CRM (customer relationship management) tool, scheduling app, reminders, or time blocking.

The time will come when you're the experienced one, and you can pass your knowledge on to the new recruits.

ACTION STEP

Make a list of the top 5–10 people who are successful in your field, and spend time learning from them.

6
ADVICE TO A NEW BROKER

It's tempting to want to "do it all." When you are first starting, you don't want opportunities to pass you by. If you specialize in one area, but an opportunity comes up in another, you miss that opportunity ... right?

Not exactly.

When you start your commercial real estate broker career, you want to hone your skills so heavily in one area that you are the go-to person every single time another broker finds that opportunity (see Step 7). When you have a team of experienced brokers, you can fall back on their experience, even when you don't have it yourself in a particular area.

When I was a new broker, I would seek opportunities. Then, after I found them, I would explain that Coldwell Banker Commercial has a team approach, so I could partner with the broker with 25 years of experience in multi-family, or the guy with 20 years of experience in industrial, or the lady with 20 years of experience in retail ... you get the idea.

Over the last seven years, I have watched my business double in size in three of those seven years. It's largely this team approach but also sticking with the systems (see Step 14), even if they don't seem to be paying off at first.

Here are the processes I advise new brokers to adopt:

- You need to be working from 8 a.m. to 6 p.m.
- Prospecting should be your highest priority; strive to set

at least five meetings per day. Ask your prospects loads of questions, and don't be afraid to pre-qualify them. One of the toughest lessons I learned was that I should not waste my time on deals that would never be deals.

- Experience cannot be gained through education, so help senior brokers as a way to get your feet wet.
- Your business is a marathon, not a sprint. Think long-term. It might mean missing a commission today so you can earn a lifelong client who will be instrumental in your success.
- If you sacrifice your ethics, you sacrifice everything. Getting a client into a bad building will put food on the table today but a bad taste in their mouth forever.
- Don't skip your morning routine. My worst days are the ones where I cut corners and slept in.

ACTION STEP

Write down your specialty, prospect like your life depends on it, and lean heavily on your senior team members when opportunities arise that are outside of your specialty.

7

SPECIALIZE

Specialists always make more money than generalists. So when trying to be an expert in everything, you end up being an expert in nothing.

At the beginning of my career, I quickly realized that I was leaning toward multi-family properties.

I already owned rental units, so it made sense to head in that direction. By focusing my efforts in this one area for a time, my name became well recognized as the go-to guy if you're buying or selling a multi-family property.

To make myself known, I did a little data farming (see Step 19). First, I went to title companies and ordered a list of all property owners with five or more units within a 60-mile radius of Billings.

With that mailing list, I created a marketing piece that wouldn't be quickly tossed in the trash.

In my letter, I introduced myself and relayed three challenges that multi-family owners experience: vacancy, bad tenants, and trying to sell their property for what they know it is worth.

Because nearly every owner experiences these challenges, it was as though I spoke directly to that one property owner.

Using the latest data farming technology (Reonomy is one of many software programs that will track down owner information for you), I contacted the owners once a month to check in. One month I would call, the next I would email, the following I would send a postcard, and so forth.

I contacted anyone who owned the properties within my specialty, and I became their resource for anything related to buying or selling multi-family properties.

Choose a specialty or focus area based on your interest and passion. You will be unstoppable when you are in your zone and having fun.

ACTION STEP

1. **Identify your specialty.**
2. **Data farm to get a list of every property or every tenant that fits your criteria (for example, national tenants, businesses with 30+ employees, or 10,000+ square-foot buildings).**
3. **Contact them one time per month via phone, email, mailing, newsletter, or sharing success stories.**

8

PUT IN THE TIME

Work like no one else is willing to work so you can live like no one else can live.

I get up at 5 a.m. to read, work out, and accomplish my most important tasks before breakfast. We are at our most productive in the morning, and we are especially productive after working out to kick-start our bodies and minds.

When my morning routine is done, I'm ready to conquer the day, and I have a full day ahead of me. If my morning started at 8 a.m., I would have three fewer hours to finish just as much, and I would miss out on that early morning productivity.

As you start out, you must develop your systems and stick with them. The key to being successful is to do both the hard and the easy things consistently. Little activities like marketing tasks are easy to do ... but they're just as easy to NOT do.

In my real estate career, I put in the time for two and a half years and fast-tracked my success using the steps in this book; many commercial real estate brokers take much longer before things really take off.

Then my success grew exponentially. The saying, "Being an entrepreneur means living a few years like most people won't so that you can spend the rest of your life like most people can't," became true.

Your morning routine, reviewing your goals, and doing what you know will work will eventually pay off. It takes three to five years to be running at full speed; once you are in it, stay in it.

ACTION STEP

Get up early in the morning to add more hours to your day. Be willing to work hard and keep working hard.

9
PROVIDE VALUE TO PROSPECTS

Your job as a real estate broker is to show that you are the expert. You do this by providing value to your potential clients.

One of the best ways to provide that value is to create a story around how you do it. Your story doesn't need to be long and can be simple, like these three recent stories of mine.

1. I recently sold an industrial building on five acres of land. It sold for more than what the owner had been told it was worth, and it sold faster than expected.
2. A retail landlord was suffering from a 50% vacancy in his building. Within three months, we located three tenants, and now the landlord's building is 100% occupied while achieving higher lease rates.
3. When a nonprofit was looking for a new location in the Billings medical corridor, I helped find the right location and a buyer for their existing building. I even found a place for them to lease to bridge the gap between selling the old building, renovating the new one, and moving into their new building.

Each little story can be a PR marketing piece pushed out to local journals, posted on social media, and more. I also customize those valuable pieces to my prospects in similar situations.

If you're just starting and you don't have these valuable stories yet, your task is to create 12 topics on commercial real estate and send out those value-adding pieces to your prospects, or even news outlets, once a month for a year.

ACTION STEP

Write or find articles already written on real estate topics and share them with your contacts. Make them applicable, interesting, and relevant.

10

SURVIVE YOUR FIRST YEAR IN REAL ESTATE

One of the scariest aspects of your first year in real estate is the idea that your income is 100% commission; you only eat what you kill. That means if you aren't making a sale, then you're not making money, and you struggle with your bills.

But we must remember that we should only sell commercial real estate from a place of confidence, not desperation. Clients can tell, and it will affect their decision to do business with you or not.

How do you act confidently when your finances hinge on making that sale?

My first-year mentor, Steve Kenney, told me, "Nate, go get a home equity line of credit, or go to the bank and get a business line of credit. Have something available so that you have a safety net. Even if you don't use it, your confidence will skyrocket knowing that it's there."

Too many entrepreneurs and real estate brokers shoot their careers in the foot by getting a second job. They steal time and energy from their chosen career and put it toward something they hate doing.

Even a small $10,000 line of credit means the difference between struggling and thriving.

In commercial real estate, transactions can take three to six months to close. You know the money is coming, but you still have to pay the monthly bills. Your line of credit will be your steady paycheck for a little while; it will put gas in your vehicle and food on your table, and your wife won't tell you to get a part-time job at McDonald's as mine did.

ACTION STEP

Take out a line of credit that will act as your safety net. Thoroughly understand your interest rate and repayment options so you don't get into financial trouble.

11

LONGEVITY IS YOUR FRIEND

I worked my tail off during my first year as a commercial real estate broker. I was knocking on doors, cold calling, and using the tactics you're reading about in this book.

One day, I talked with a prospect who was very interested in selling his property. A few days later, George Warmer (who became one of my mentors) walked into our morning team meeting and had the listing from the seller I had just spoken with.

Later, I asked Blaine Poppler, another of my mentors, why I didn't land that listing. Blaine looked me in the eye and said, "Nate, longevity is your friend."

Pick a good organization and stay with it. Successful brokers make more money when their clients always know where to find them instead of trying to figure out which firm they are at now.

If you switch companies, even though you're still selling commercial real estate, all your clients must find you again. Your email and mailing addresses have changed; you have a new logo and are hard to find.

The grass isn't always greener on the other side. That change will set your career back two to three years.

Longevity also has a compound effect when you apply it to other organizations that you are involved in. Some of my best clients have come from attending my weekly BNI business networking group, monthly Chamber of Commerce events, regularly volunteering at my church, and sitting on the board of directors at my kids' school. Your community involvement on a consistent basis will drastically improve your relationship and business success.

It takes three to five years to master your craft. Good brokers experience the hockey stick curve at that point, and their business takes off like a rocket ship. Then you start gaining repeat business, and referral leads come in.

ACTION STEP

Choose an organization with the culture and values you love. Research them now so you don't shoot your career in the foot by switching companies down the road.

12

INCREASE YOUR COMMERCIAL REAL ESTATE KNOWLEDGE

If you want a Level 10 career, you must first be a Level 10 broker. Getting there comes from education and experience.

For those who are just starting, you have all the educational resources in the world at your fingertips. Experience will come with time; I'll show you how to expedite it in the next section.

First, take the CCIM 101 course ASAP.

The Certified Commercial Investment Member designation is like earning your master's degree in commercial real estate.

All four courses will take a couple of years to complete. As you work on those courses, read the books *The Book on Investing in Real Estate with No (and Low) Money Down* by Brandon Turner, and *Brokers Who Dominate* by Rod Santomassimo. Both books will complement the knowledge from CCIM courses as you learn creative ways to make a transaction happen, including using seller financing or a seller carryback.

Earning your CCIM will leapfrog you into the top 10% of all commercial real estate brokers. When a broker from out of state has a referral for someone in your area, they are far more likely to choose those with this designation.

There are plenty of ways to increase your knowledge. When I first joined Coldwell Banker Commercial, I saw David Mitchell working closely with Starbucks to track down ideal locations in our state.

I asked him how it was going, and he explained that he didn't just look at actively listed properties. Instead, he furthered his education outside of what an average commercial real estate broker looks at. He learned how to use demographic tools, traffic count tools, and other sophisticated software that a client of that caliber required to find the perfect site.

Increasing knowledge sets you apart from the crowd.

ACTION STEP

Sign up for a CCIM course, read commercial real estate books, and talk to your more experienced colleagues.

13

PERSONAL INVESTMENT IN REAL ESTATE

Have you heard the phrase, "Never trust a skinny chef?" People will buy more real estate from someone who has ***lived*** every opportunity and every challenge that comes with real estate.

It's not enough to only know about it or understand it. That experience ensures you can answer questions your clients will inevitably have.

- Have you completed a remodel and know the challenges?
- Have you had to evict bad tenants?
- Have you failed – or been held up – when trying to complete a remodel for a tenant of a commercial space?
- Do you know what construction and remodels cost?
- Have you been through the permitting process with the city for new construction? For a remodel?
- Have you cut big checks to architects and engineers during a build-to-suit?
- Do you know the pains of having a vacancy and the value of a reserve account?
- Do you have war stories that your clients can use to make educated decisions or know that you are the right man or woman for the job?

My brother-in-law and I bought an older commercial building at a dramatically reduced price. It looked like a no-brainer.

Over a year later, after having all five units completely overhauled (including new sewer lines, electrical service, updating to ADA compliance, and more), the building was ready for tenants. It was no longer that fire sale of a price tag, but we both learned what happens when just about *everything* goes wrong.

ACTION STEP

Find a real estate venture that will give you hands-on experience.

Part II

UNSTOPPABLE GROWTH

14
SYSTEMS FOR GROWING YOUR BUSINESS CONSISTENTLY

You must have a system to grow your network. Many tasks are easy to accomplish, and when they're easy to do, they're just as easy to NOT do.

Putting the right system in place will make these tasks easier, more efficient, and turnkey. When times are great, you do them. When times are slow, you do them. This activity will get you off the roller-coaster of feast or famine; mine has seen consistent year-over-year growth, which is an accomplishment that few business owners get to enjoy.

- Set your weekly reminder to schedule one to three networking lunches or coffees with those who touch or refer commercial real estate (see Step 16).
- Set your weekly reminder to add all new contacts to Facebook, an email distribution list, LinkedIn, your CRM, etc.
- Set your weekly reminder to review and update listings on marketing websites, and be sure to renew the listing contracts when needed (see Step 36).
- Set a reminder to contact past clients (two to four times per year).
- Schedule one week of social media posts for the next week (weekly).

- Email marketing to past clients (four times a year).
- Email marketing to referral partners (four times a year).
- Reminder to schedule two to three networking events per week.
- Monthly reminder to call on FSBO properties (Craigslist, signs around town, etc.).
- Monthly mailings reminder – this could be handwritten thank-you notes or cards, data farming (see Step 19), or advertising a new property for sale/lease to targeted tenants/buyers or landlords.
- Weekly/monthly reminder to stop by and chat it up with past clients to generate new referrals.
- Yearly reminder to email all your contacts with a "year in review" email, recapping your previous year to let them know you are growing and doing big things.
- Weekly or monthly reminder to make warm/cold calls on your commercial real estate specialty. One of my colleagues does this in a one-to-four-hour time block, calling on retail developers for national tenants or to those national tenants themselves.

You need a system of recurring reminders, and executing such reminders will ensure your database and pipeline are continually growing.

I used a calendar program (Outlook) to stay on top of these activities and was able to grow my numbers from $2.5 million in my first year to $50-plus million in my seventh year.

Tailor this to your style and add the most effective items, such as weekly Facebook live videos. When you get too busy to keep up with these, either delegate activities to your assistant, or allow them to hound you until you complete them.

ACTION STEP

Find and set up a CRM system to create *reminders* — daily, weekly, monthly, quarterly, and yearly. Review and complete them consistently (especially when you don't feel like it).

15
OUTSOURCE ADMIN AND MARKETING TASKS

About a year into my commercial real estate broker career, I found I was getting overwhelmed by the aspects of running a business instead of getting out there and selling. So I followed popular advice and found a virtual assistant from the Philippines.

At first, everything was great. But over time, quality and consistency dropped off. Finally, I had to have a difficult conversation because all I had done was create more work for myself.

I realized I needed to hire someone with a complementing skill set to my own.

So, I hired my current assistant, Cindy Tapp. Cindy lives five states away in the Chicagoland area. She is a stay-at-home mom who wants to help provide for her family but doesn't want to get just any job. She started at two hours per day and now works three to four hours per day as she streamlines the efficiency of my business. She is detail-oriented and has the organization skills that jive with my vision and expertise in real estate.

Cindy helps with social media, email marketing, quarterly email newsletters to past clients, adding contacts to my database, sending mailings to past clients (or to a geographic area I am "farming"), and other repetitive marketing/admin tasks. I don't have to worry or micromanage her, and she has my complete trust, even access to my credit cards, so she can pay for ads and more.

Over time, I discovered that Cindy's motivation and quality of work directly correlate to how much vision I impart to her. When

I'm not imparting the vision, she has to guess what I'm thinking and what my expectations are for her. To help with this, we have a celebration phone call every Friday where we celebrate successes. Her achievements are directly related to my own, and together we can celebrate as a successful team.

Many task management apps are available to set up a system to delegate and track tasks that you are assigning to your assistant. I initially set up my system in Asana, costing me about $25 a month. However, other equally efficient apps are available, such as Monday.com, Zoho Projects, Kintone, and Trello. Read the book *Virtual Freedom* by Chris Ducker to get ideas about how to set up a perfect system for hiring a virtual assistant who can live anywhere and produce high-quality work for you.

ACTION STEP

Hire an assistant, impart your vision, and be specific about your systems and processes so they can replicate them. Then you can rest assured the work is getting done on a regular basis and your time is freed up for building relationships with your clients.

16
NETWORK YOUR WAY TO SUCCESS

When I lived in Chicago, I ran an energy brokerage business. I quickly learned that if I wanted to catch the big fish, I had to fish in the pond where the big fish swam.

Over time, you will connect with them, but only if you see them regularly.

When you're networking, it's not about how many people you can bombard and shove your info into their hands. Instead, it's more important to see how many people you can form a true and deep relationship with.

A few good relationships far outweigh handing out a hundred business cards and walking away with an awkward feeling.

When I first came to Billings, I joined BNI. A painter was in that group, and I developed a deep relationship with him. Six years later, long after leaving the group, he called me up. He explained that as a painter, he meets a lot of commercial real estate brokers, but I was the only one he wanted to do business with.

When he explained what he needed, I realized it was a perfect match for a listing I had that was over two years old. That relationship, developed years prior, resulted in two happy clients from the transaction.

Join networking groups; find your people. Here is a list of some of the groups I have been a part of over the years.

- BNI - bni.com
- Rotary Club International - rotary.org/en
- Your local Chamber of Commerce
- SCORE - score.org
- Entrepreneurs' Organization - hub.eonetwork.org

ACTION STEP

Join networking groups where you will meet the clients you want to work with. Attend at least two or three meetings each week.

17
WORK BY REFERRAL

Read the books *Work by Referral* by Brian Buffini and Joe Niego, and *Seven Levels of Communication* by Michael Maher. Together, they will outline the exact tasks you need to do to produce consistent referrals.

One of the most powerful connection tools you can make is a handwritten note. Society has essentially become "allergic" to writing handwritten notes; if you put in the 5 or 10 minutes per day it takes to write a few of them, you are immediately light years ahead of your peers.

Check-in calls are just as easy. Call the client when you drive past a building you sold or leased. Let them know you're just checking in to ensure everything is working well for them. It only takes a few of those calls before a referral comes from them.

The more infrequent the activity, the bigger it should be. Quarterly and yearly parties should have some planning behind them. Make them fun events that people want to go to.

Daily:

1. Write three personal notes
2. Make five check-in calls
3. Add one person to your database

Weekly:

1. Host two business lunches
2. Average at least 10 pop-bys
3. Attend at least one networking meeting

Monthly:

1. Send an item of value to your entire database
2. Make personal contact with A+ clients
3. Attend a social or business networking event

Quarterly:

1. Host a networking party, seminar, or gathering
2. Update your business directory or database

Yearly:

1. Host a party for your A+ clients
2. Get support for your business

Two people recently referred me to the same large industrial listing. Upon a successful transaction, I called each referral partner and updated them on how the landlord of this building was extremely satisfied, I had exceeded expectations, and they had a great new tenant.

One of the biggest mistakes I have noticed commercial real estate brokers make is that they do a phenomenal job at generating referrals, but they fail to circle back with their referral partners to communicate their success and say thank you.

Always update partners, thank them for the referrals, and prove that you're worth continuing to be referred.

ACTION STEP

Implement regular tasks daily, weekly, monthly, quarterly, and yearly to generate referrals and to follow up with referral partners. Be consistent.

18
BUILD A KILLER DATABASE

"He or she with the best database wins."

You have probably heard the phrase, "It's not what you know; it's who you know."

There is more to the concept than just knowing people. You must also be in constant and consistent communication with your database.

When I first moved to Billings, I didn't even know 10 people. However, I had a laser-like focus on adding people to my database. Using networking groups, social media, and just finding people I wanted to get to know, I built a relationship with them, added them to my database, and stayed in touch.

Today, I probably know one-tenth of the number of people that Todd Sherman (a senior broker in our office) knows. He knows way more people, way more affluent people, and he has the longevity that builds trust. But he didn't organize his database for consistent communication. I'm happy to report that once he read this secret playbook, his database became well organized, it grew, and it turned into referrals and transactions.

This is how I did it:

- Create an Excel spreadsheet or use a CRM to track every transaction you have completed, including client contact details – name, address, and phone. Call or email past clients at least four times each year to stay in touch.
- Add everyone you meet to Facebook, LinkedIn, or Instagram. Posting your new listings to social media so

you stay top of mind with all your contacts is a great way to generate referrals.

- Create an email list of referral partners (bankers, attorneys, CPAs, people in your networking group, etc.) and send them an email marketing blast with all your listings four times a year.
- Create your own real estate brokers list within your chosen CRM, and add all the commercial real estate brokers to it. Don't be afraid to add residential brokers, as they can be good referral partners. Contact them with every new listing you land.
- Go meet 100 people in 100 days, and your business will take off immediately. Put everyone in your database and follow up diligently.

ACTION STEP

A ton of great CRM (customer relationship management) tools are out there. Find one that works and add ALL the people to it. Then, use it!

19
DATA FARM TO DOMINATE

What separates an average real estate broker from the top producers? It's how many properties they have access to. Average real estate brokers only expose their clients to 5% to 10% of the properties actively listed on the market. On the other hand, the top producers connect their clients with the other 90% to 95% of unlisted properties.

When I started my real estate journey, I asked the seasoned brokers about their experience with mailings. Nearly all of them said, "It's not worth your time." I quickly learned that it was because they had not approached it the right way.

At the time, I was heavily focused on my specialty, multi-family listings. I noticed two major problems plaguing this market: vacancies and bad tenants.

Using the three tools in the following bulleted list, I could find the owner information for every multi-family property within 60 miles of Billings. I crafted a letter that addressed these issues and added the owners to my database.

The results were that within a year, not a single property owner who fit my qualifications didn't know my name.

- Looking to get a tenant rep assignment for all the law firms with over 25 employees? Use https://datavu.databaseusa.com/home. Datavu creates a prospect list based on whatever parameters you put in.
- Looking for contact details for all the multi-family owners within your city? Use www.reonomy.com. Reonomy will

give you all the known contact details for the property type you're searching for.
- Looking to connect with all commercial property owners in your city? Contact local title companies to get a list of their mailing addresses.

Most commercial real estate brokers don't even realize all the tools they can use to connect buyers, sellers, and tenants with commercial real estate opportunities. For almost any assignment, there is a data farming tactic that you can use to produce superior results.

ACTION STEP

You only know who you know; start data farming to build your killer database and rapidly expand your reach.

20

TOP 20 WHALES

Perry Marshall wrote about the 80/20 principle. Simplified, it states that 80% of your sales come from 20% of your clients.

Early in my career, I noticed that it took about as much work to perform a small real estate transaction as it did a larger one. I realized that if I was spending the time, I needed to spend the time on the ones that would bring in the most revenue.

I sat down and put together a list of the top 20 prospects or referral partners I wanted to be in front of consistently. Because if you spend your time working with these whales, the 80/20 principle says that it won't take long to increase your income five-fold.

But it doesn't stop with one list.

Every year, usually around Christmas or the first of the year, I review every transaction I did the previous year. I organize them into the largest 20% and the smallest 80%.

Then I go through each client in that 20% and ask myself, "How did I get the referral for this transaction? How do I get in front of more of these kinds of clients?" That obsession has led to double- or triple-digit growth in my career every year.

List your top 20 "whale" clients and set reminders to call on them monthly or quarterly. Know who has money and can immediately execute any great deal you put in front of them. Review this list regularly as a memory jogger about what kinds of deals you should be working on and who you should be talking to.

ACTION STEP

Make your top 20 list, consistently contact that list, and refine that list at least once a year to bring in the most revenue.

21

GO-GIVERS SELL MORE

In one of my first sales jobs, I had a boss who couldn't get through the day without her "daily dose of cigarettes, Red Bull, and lies."

I wish that were an exaggeration or a joke, but she was the incarnation of a sleazy salesperson. Seeing her in action left a bad taste in my mouth and the client's mouth, and I was determined to run my business in the exact opposite manner.

Read the book called *The Go-Giver*, then read the sequel called *Go-Givers Sell More*, and read many of my top 30 books in this guide.

One common theme is that the more you give, the more you receive. This is the law of reciprocity at its finest.

- Statistically speaking, you will need to give 100 referrals to receive 50 referrals.
- Always look to connect good people. If someone is looking for a contractor or service provider, be the first to say, "I have a guy I can introduce you to!" or "Let me introduce you to Sarah; I don't trust anyone else with XYZ."
- Provide so much value that a new client would never consider using another real estate broker. Give clients expert advice, based on killer data, without expecting anything in return.
- You may occasionally have someone pump you for information and then go it alone. Still, most people will become extremely loyal to you – those are the ones who you want to work with, after all.

- The world does not operate in a finite space. You can create an immense amount of goodwill by connecting two people who would enjoy meeting each other and benefit from the relationship. Giving a referral is an easy way to provide value.

ACTION STEP

Read the *Go-Giver* books. Keep a list of partners who you regularly refer to others. Add value without expecting anything in return.

22

SPEND 50% OF YOUR TIME ON DOLLAR-PRODUCTIVE ACTIVITIES

How do you know what a dollar-productive activity is when you are brand new to the business? How do you know what activities will lead to new listings, new buyers, selling properties, or anything that will ultimately make you money?

At first, I would start the day with easy tasks. I filled my mornings with admin duties, marketing tasks, redesigning brochures, shooting off random emails, and other things that took time but ultimately didn't land new opportunities.

If you sit in the office more than 50% of the day, you won't make it in real estate.

You should be spending as much as 75% of your time as a new broker at networking groups, making phone calls to everyone in your database, calling for-sale-by-owners, stopping by past clients' homes or places of work, writing handwritten notes to your contacts, taking referral partners out for coffee or lunch, handing out fliers to all the adjacent property owners on your new listing, and anything that puts you eyeball-to-eyeball with a small-business owner or investor to talk real estate. Ask them if they know of anyone having trouble finding a good piece of commercial real estate or if they know any small-business owners looking to expand.

My dollar-productive hours go from 8 a.m. to 3 p.m., where I'm making calls, setting up meetings, doing pop-bys, and going to lunch with referral partners. Then, by 3 p.m. when the day has slowed, I fulfill all the work I created for myself.

New brokers invest a lot of time in making a perfect brochure or researching a client. Ideally, spend most of your time physically doing the activities that create opportunity.

ACTION STEP

Identify and list your top three to five most important dollar-productive activities. Spend 75% of your time on these activities. Avoid sitting in the office for too long.

23

YOU ARE THE AVERAGE OF THE FIVE PEOPLE YOU SPEND THE MOST TIME WITH

Jim Rohn tells us that we are the average of the five people we spend the most time with.

Who are you hanging out with? How can you improve your circle of influence?

Before I even got into real estate, I had big real estate ambitions. And I found that the more time I spent with people doing bigger and better things, the more drive I had to do bigger and better things too.

And that meant some of my friends since grade school started to drop off. They're good people, but they have W2 jobs they hate, slog through the workweek so they can party all weekend long, and then complain about not having any vacation time.

The more time I spent with the heavy hitters, the less time I had for those who only brought me down.

There's more to it than that. If you consume content on social media that isn't empowering you, it's bringing you down. Instead, choose to consume only that which will drive you forward.

Review your relationships every six months and prioritize them based on your relationship and their status as a decision-maker. Then concentrate on the top contacts.

ACTION STEP

Take a hard look at where you spend your time. List five people you need to spend more time with. Spending more time with the empowering automatically means less time with the disempowering.

24

GROW YOUR MARKET PRESENCE

Growing your market presence is all about "bragging" about the things you have done. But you must frame it right to ensure you're not bragging about yourself; instead, you brag about your clients.

Tell the story of a successful or large transaction. Thank your clients for letting you help them find the right place.

Tell the success story that now, with the right real estate in place, their big dreams can continue to surge forward.

This story is all about them; you're the supporting cast.

- Write articles for local newspapers and real estate publications.
- Sit on panels and boards that include other real estate professionals.
- Market yourself. When you have a success (closing a big deal), ask your marketing department to create a press release and post it to social media, send a deal announcement postcard to prospects or existing clients, and more.
- Help other brokers in your office. A rising tide raises all ships.
- Reinvent yourself! Stay on top of trends in your business. When there is a drastic market shift, go where the money is. Be a leader who is in the know, and stay in front of the competition.

By placing the focus on the client, you can communicate your success while staying humble in the process.

ACTION STEP

Identify three ways to share success stories. Market yourself by telling these stories where your clients are the stars. Make sure it couldn't have been done without you, but they are the focus.

25

DO AS MUCH HOMEWORK ON A PROSPECTIVE CLIENT AS POSSIBLE

Dan Mathews, a senior commercial real estate broker, is the stealth bomber of real estate prospecting.

When he wanted to get in with the CEO of a big bank here in town, he started with that CEO's assistant.

Through mutual connections, he discovered she loved a local T-shirt company. So he bought a couple of shirts, mailed them to the office, and included a note that said, "Look forward to connecting soon. - D" No name, no other info, just his first initial.

He then looked into the details about the CEO and discovered he was fascinated with an old, expensive Scotch whisky. He found a bottle and sent it to the CEO, including a note saying, "We'll be in touch. - D"

Now the assistant and CEO were curious, wondering who this mysterious D was who knew exactly what they loved. Dan waited a week and then called, saying, "Hi, I'm Dan; I'm calling to see if you received my packages."

His immediate "in" got him an appointment with the CEO.

Be creative with your outreach. Have fun with it, and personalize it to those big prospects with whom you want to connect.

With the availability of information today, there is no reason you should not be able to make a call and tell your prospect something that they do not know about their industry or topic of interest.

Just don't make it creepy, of course.

ACTION STEP

Thoroughly research your client before meeting with them. Find something to share that will impress them.

26
CAN I BUY YOU LUNCH?

You have **780 Food and Drink Opportunities per year**.

Most of your referrals will come from those with whom you have developed a personal relationship. This happens when you break bread with them, share your life, and really get to know them.

I have two to three lunches per week, two to three coffees per week, and a happy hour beer here and there. These consistent meetings are with people I know will help me to grow my business or those who provide a valuable service to my clients – bankers, attorneys, surveyors, etc.

What if you can't afford multiple lunches, coffees, and beers every week? Then you have two options.

The first method is one I don't recommend you rely on. But many of those you will meet have funds set aside for business lunches, and they will offer to pay for the meal. Again, don't *expect* it to happen, but it often does.

Second, build that relationship after finding your prospect and then calling them. Ask them if you can pop in for 15 to 20 minutes because you're impressed with how successful they are. Tell them you want to learn about their business, discover what makes them successful, and get to know them so you can hopefully refer business to them.

People rarely turn down the opportunity to brag about themselves and get more referrals.

Your connections will help you become your city's most-referred real estate broker.

ACTION STEP

Identify how many food and drink opportunities you are currently taking advantage of. Commit to a system to ensure they happen more regularly moving forward.

27

TOP 100 LIST

When I first started in the business, I thought to myself, "How can I ensure that I'm constantly in front of anyone who is influential, has money, is a small-business owner, has invested in real estate, or otherwise would be a great client?"

I know that what you focus on is what you get. If you focus on not losing – you lose; if you focus on winning – you win.

I created the top 100 list: the top 100 people who would make great clients or referral partners. I then took steps to become strategically connected to them.

After meeting them in person, I added them to my social media circles. I would get their information into my database and connect with them via email marketing.

This list isn't about selling to people but about planting seeds. I may have connected with them in my first year, but it wasn't until several years later, consistently seeing success stories, that they felt comfortable referring business to me.

Most people know a hundred residential real estate brokers but almost no commercial real estate brokers.

Business is about relationships, and sometimes you must seek out those relationships as they often don't just fall into your lap. Tell everyone you talk to who you are looking to meet. You never know who might be able to help you out!

ACTION STEP

List the top 100 people you want to meet. Seek them out, ask others for an introduction, and learn how you can be a resource for them.

28

YOU ARE THE MOST IMPORTANT PERSON IN MY LIFE

People crave genuine connections.

When you can connect personally, the rest of the business activities become very, very easy.

Much of it starts with how you answer the phone. Eventually, clients catch on, and it turns into a little game, like when I get a call from Jamie.

Nate: "Hey, Jamie."

Jamie: "What's up, boss?"

Nate: "I'm not the boss; you're the boss!"

We have our routine; it lightens the mood and ultimately makes things more fun and enjoyable.

The more you can find creative ways to let someone know they are the most important person to you, the more you will connect and enjoy long-term success.

When they ask if you have time for them, you respond, "I always have time for you. What's up?"

Or say something corny like, "Hey, I've been waiting for your call all day! What took you so long?"

Treat each client like they are your only client and make the people you deal with look good, especially in front of their boss.

ACTION STEP

List ways to let your clients know you *always* have time for them because each one is your most important client.

PART III

THE MOST-REFERRED BROKER

29

BULLETPROOF YOUR TRANSACTION

I bulletproof transactions by creating a roadmap of what to expect and how to solve problems – before they become problems. This is made possible with a strong outgoing referral network.

I was helping a client sell his $4 million mini-storage facility. But before the sale could go through, he had to subdivide the land to separate his personal house from the mini-storage facility. We were on a tight timeline, and the surveyor we hired initially couldn't get it done.

Knowing this could delay the deal by six months, I jumped in and reached out to an engineer who had surveying and subdividing as one of their specialties. I connected the two, and they worked quickly to record the new plat and close the deal.

In every transaction, I give the clients a roadmap of what to expect throughout the process. Knowing the property, the buyer, and the seller means I foresee snags. I can remedy them long before we even get to that point in the roadmap.

This allows me to speed up a transaction and control the outcome of the due diligence process. My trusted referral partners include:

- Architect
- Engineer

- Surveyor
- Environmental Consultant (Phase 1 and Phase 2)
- Eviction Attorney
- Real Estate Attorney
- Property Inspector
- Banker
- Appraiser
- Insurance Agent
- Roofer
- Windows and Siding
- Electrician
- Plumber (including scoping sewer lines)
- HVAC
- Painter
- Flooring
- Handyman
- Asphalt/Paving
- Tree Service and Removal
- Title Company

To make things go even quicker, I not only give the name of the referral partner, but I make the introduction by email. Then, building up both sides, I explain the need and why I trust the partner to do the job quickly.

ACTION STEP

Make a list of trusted professionals who serve a specific purpose in the transaction process. Regularly make targeted introductions as beneficial during a real estate transaction.

30
BE REMARKABLE

Every client expects you to take them to the closing table.

If that's where the transaction ends, you've done the minimum for your job; you haven't become remarkable.

Your goal is to be so good that your clients want to "share" you and how competent you are with others. To achieve this, go above and beyond so clients rave about their past transactions with you.

A good broker can get a deal to the finish line. A great broker is always sure to give their client a little something extra – it's the unexpected surprise that makes you remarkable. Give your client a best-in-class thank-you gift at closing – often worth 5% of your net commissions.

So many companies out there brand cheap pens, cheap coffee mugs, and cheap junk, making their name synonymous with being cheap. Instead, brand your name with the best of the best.

I love to give gifts such as Yeti coolers, Yeti mugs, custom-engraved pocketknives, Dom Perignon, Cristal Champaign, top-shelf whiskey, and Bose mini speakers for the golf course.

The key to a great gift is to have it highly tailored to their interests and passions. For the golfer, it's an accessory monogrammed with their initials or something so extra they would never buy it for themselves.

I like to give my clients a gift right when we are walking out of a big closing, and I get to tell them I have just one more surprise for them.

I estimate that 99% of your competition thinks their job is done once the papers are signed, and they forget to secure a lifetime of referrals with that little extra surprise.

ACTION STEP

Always have a "remarkable" gift ready for your clients so you stand out as the best of the best in their minds. Read the book *Giftology* by John Ruhlin for more details on this idea.

31
BECOME A LISTING MACHINE

Your listing clients will bring in more money, with less effort, than your buying clients.

When you represent a buyer and are making an offer on a highly sought-after property that is currently listed, you often have less than a 50% chance of winning the deal; there's a lot of competition on the really good properties that hit the market, and this will drastically reduce your odds of getting an offer accepted. When you list a very desirable property, however, the chances of completing the transaction soar to 90% or higher. The senior brokers around our office have a famous saying: "List to Last."

Using a data farm (see Step 19), you can find and export details for every commercial real estate owner.

Then, you can send regular mailings (see Steps 14 and 15). Remember, a single touch rarely works; 4 to 12 times per year is necessary.

I had many prospects file my mailings away and then contact me years later with a need. Maybe their broker wasn't working out, retired, or passed away. Sometimes they just needed someone in my specialty (see Step 7), and I was the right person for the job.

Many brokers will cap out at 10 to 15 listings, thinking they made it. However, when I put the right systems and checklists in place (see Step 36), I could manage as many as 40 to 50 listings at a time.

Reviewing my business each year, I employed the 80/20 principle (see Step 20) to further refine my listings to only focus on those that bring in the most business.

ACTION STEP

Review your current processes to acquire listings. Use a data farm to fill your database. Create a marketing process that includes regular mailings to ensure sellers have your contact details when they are ready to list.

32
AVOID AND OUTSOURCE

You simplify, delegate, and eliminate tasks in your business that aren't moving you to your goal. Do the same in your personal life.

Lengthy personal chores that take you away from your business or family life should be outsourced. For example, you can hire a neighborhood teen to mow your lawn for $15 to $20 per hour. When you're rising to the top of your real estate career, it's no longer worth doing it on your own.

If your sink or toilet is broken in your house, hire a plumber. If your car breaks down, hire a mechanic.

Don't try to take on a whole new skill set to avoid spending a little money. Instead, refocus that time on something that will make you more money.

Figure out your average hourly rate and outsource all tasks that you can pay someone else less per hour than what you make.

Because if you can make more as a plumber, you might be in the wrong business!

ACTION STEP

Determine your hourly rate (yearly income divided by 2080). Identify and outsource any task that someone else can do cheaper to free up more of your time.

33
BE AN EXPERT IN SELLER FINANCING

In my second year in the business, I had a listing for an office/retail building that had been lingering on the market with a price tag of $1.5 million. When a developer approached with an offer of $1 million – the maximum amount their bank would approve – I knew the seller wouldn't reduce the sale by half a million dollars.

Instead, we negotiated a deal for $1.3 million. We used the first million from the bank, and the seller financed the other $300K. It turned into a win/win for everyone involved.

Did the appraisal come up short on a commercial property? Have the seller provide seller financing in the second position behind the bank to make up the difference between the purchase price and the appraisal.

Does the seller not want to sell because they'll lose their residual income? Have them provide seller financing so they continue to enjoy residual income without the headaches of dealing with tenants.

Is the seller's accountant saying that by selling a property, they will get put into a higher tax bracket? Have the seller sell the property on a contract for deed and take a small down payment along with monthly payments over time to spread out their tax liability.

Do you know what a contract for deed is? Do you know what a note and trust indenture is?

A contract for deed is a contract for the sale of property that provides the buyer will acquire possession of the land immediately and pay the purchase price in installments over a period of time; however, the seller will retain legal title until all payments are made.

A trust deed is always used together with a promissory note that sets out the amount and terms of the loan. The property owner signs the note, which is a written promise to repay the borrowed money. A trust deed then gives the third-party "trustee" (usually a title company) legal ownership of the property.

Seller financing is one of my secret weapons for getting deals done because the opportunities are endless. Become an expert and enjoy doing way more deals and potentially even acquiring more properties, with less money down, for yourself.

ACTION STEP

Read the book *The Book on Investing in Real Estate with No (and Low) Money Down* by Brandon Turner. Learn all the ways to be creative with financing options. Find a good real estate attorney who can draft seller financing documents for your client.

34
RISK–REWARD SPECTRUM IN REAL ESTATE

Commercial real estate falls into four buckets based on how much risk a client is willing to take.

- Low Risk, Lowest Reward – buy and hold properties
- Medium Risk, Medium Reward – value-add properties
- High Risk, High Reward – development or redevelopment
- Highest Risk, Highest Reward – land development

You can make the most ideal suggestions by knowing your client and understanding which properties fit their risk tolerance.

I recently had a client sell his mini-storage facility. It was extremely low maintenance and a cash cow; he got top dollar for it. After the sale, he was forced to make a decision: should he reinvest the profits or pay taxes on the sale?

We came up with the strategy that since he had a high tolerance for risk, he would achieve the highest returns doing raw land development. He bought large tracts of land, subdivided them, went through the zoning process, and created an industrial park on spec. Each building had a single triple net lease tenant. He made money by developing the land and doubled up his income by renting out the buildings.

This is one example of how you can find new opportunities by knowing your client's risk tolerance level.

By explaining these four levels of real estate investment to all my clients, I quickly figure out their risk tolerance so I can put the right opportunities in front of them. This builds trust and solidifies a long-term relationship.

ACTION STEP

Review your listings and identify which risk–reward bucket each one fits into. List your clients and connect their tolerance with each bucket to discover opportunities.

35
GIVE MORE VALUE THAN YOU TAKE IN PAYMENT

Too many brokers start their business with the mindset, "How can I do as little as possible and collect as much commission as possible?" The result is making money, but is far from creating an unstoppable and fulfilling career.

To find great success, you always have to give more than you take in payment. This is done by:

- Standing out from the crowd (see Step 30).
- Read the book *Giftology*. Upon completing a successful transaction, go above and beyond and give your client a gift equal to 5% of your commission (see Step 30).
- Give your client the playbook. Guide them through the process (see Step 29). You would be amazed at how many real estate brokers put a property under contract and then leave the due diligence to chance.
- Offer to call the local media and tell them about the exciting business you worked with by finding their new location (see Steps 24 and 38).
- When your client calls and asks if you are busy, and you are crazy busy, say, "I always have time for you! How can I help?" (See Step 28.)
- Always do what you say you are going to do. Nothing ruins your credibility more than not following up – even

if you don't know how it will help you make money. Always ask people how you can help them or add value, even if it has nothing to do with real estate.

- Always return phone calls within a few hours or as soon as possible. Following up right away is the best way to do more business. In a world where "ghosting" is common, set yourself apart by following up promptly.

Every single transaction comes with a handful of referrals to ensure the entire process is seen completely through. Every interaction answers the question, "How can I add value to this relationship?"

ACTION STEP

List the top seven ways that you provide more value to your client than you take in payment. Always look for even more ways to add value to others' lives.

36

LEVERAGE SYSTEMS TO ENJOY SUCCESS

Most brokers can't handle more than 10 to 15 listings; at this point, their heads might be spinning trying to keep up.

When I first joined the business, even my mentor couldn't handle more than 25 listings. He had a great career and always saw success, but he never burst through that plateau into record-setting success.

I discovered that if I wanted to break through that plateau, I needed the following systems and checklists to ensure things got done quickly and accurately.

- Have automated (or paper) checklists for every new listing, letter of intent, due diligence, accepted offer, closing, etc. I use my CRM and daily task checklists to stay organized, with the help of my assistant.
- Use the technology available to you. For example, some CRM programs include a dialer system to automate your calls to your database. You can also create a marketing checklist for new listings in your CRM. Outlook has recurring reminders for important daily, weekly, quarterly, and yearly tasks you need to remember.
- Become a master at electronic signatures and DocuSign instead of chasing clients around the city. Use the e-sign feature for all your tech-savvy clients.

When times are slow, I maintain 25 listings. We (my assistant Cindy and I) have such a tight system and a checklist for everything that I am confident I could handle 60 listings and keep up.

ACTION STEP

Identify the top three systems you can implement that will give you more time in your day while producing better results. Find the right technology to work for you with recurring reminders, automated calls, and electronic signatures.

37

BE A PROBLEM SOLVER, NOT A SALESPERSON

My personality is to be a helper and a giver. So when I watched sales movies, such as *The Boiler Room*, *Glengarry Glen Ross*, or *The Wolf of Wall Street*, I never felt connected with the "salesperson" ideal. Finally, I realized it's because people don't want to be sold to; they want their problems solved.

If you want to make millions of dollars, all you must do is figure out what kind of real estate problem your clients have and then solve it.

When I transitioned my mindset from one where I was selling real estate to one where I was solving problems, I became far more comfortable in my career.

I even go so far as to say that I'm doing them a disservice by not calling or stopping in.

Taking the approach of a problem solver opens up their trust. Suddenly, we're not just talking business; we're having a heart-to-heart. We're building trust and a relationship.

ACTION STEP

List the problems you solve in your market better than any other real estate broker. Put a system in place to communicate your solutions to prospects and clients.

38
ADVERTISE YOUR SUCCESS

If you were the absolute best artist in the world but never displayed your art, how would anyone ever know about you?

In business, you can be the best commercial real estate broker, but if nobody hears about your success, how do they know you're really good at what you do?

Part of my systems (see Step 24) is to advertise the successes of my clients. Without bragging, I congratulate my clients on their success and thank them for allowing me to help them find the right property.

Every Tuesday, we do Testimonial Tuesday. We share pictures and five-star reviews on social media. Now people are seeing my clients' success (with my help). They want that kind of success, and they know I can help them achieve it.

ACTION STEP

Create a weekly system to advertise your clients' success and show off your own success at the same time.

CONCLUSION

If your goal is to experience success beyond your wildest dreams, it all boils down to three major themes.

1: Always give more value than you take in payment.

Most people see any business as cutthroat or dog-eat-dog. It's all about getting what you can and then moving on to the next one.

But when you take the time to deliver far more in value than you take in payment, you build relationships that last a lifetime. You consider, "If this client were signing a check for $10,000 or more and handing it to me, how much work would I put in for that payment?"

This customer service is becoming rarer and rarer as more people try to collect the most money for the least amount of work.

Set yourself apart by doing more than expected.

2: Become an expert at creating the perfect systems for success.

When I look around the office, I see many talented people who are way better real estate brokers than me. They're better salespeople, better brokers, and know more people than I do. That meant I had a different hurdle to jump over to find even more success.

I didn't achieve the top producer status because I knew a lot of people. It's because I systematized every aspect possible to create a workflow that produced endless referrals, consistent listings, and perfect marketing.

Everything flows through that system, from the data farm to the closing, so the business continues to grow year after year in an unstoppable fashion.

3: Never stop learning; never stop growing.

Did you know that 42% of people never read another book after they graduate from college?

I would never have made it in this business if I hadn't read and applied the books I talk about in this guide. Before beginning my commercial real estate journey, I discovered that the key to continued success is to constantly be learning something new – new skills, new marketing tactics, etc.

Looking back over the last 10 to 15 years, you can see that what used to work in the past isn't always going to work in the future.

So, every morning in that Miracle Morning time, read something new. Develop yourself and your business, and learn about real estate.

When you provide immense value as an expert in your specialty, and you have committed to never stop learning and growing, then you're ready for unstoppable growth.

RECOMMENDED READING LIST

Mindset and Habits

1. *The Miracle Morning: The Not-So-Obvious Secret Guaranteed to Transform Your Life – Before 8AM* by Hal Elrod (2012)
2. *Extreme Ownership: How U.S. Navy SEALs Lead and Win* by Jocko Willink and Leif Babin, et al. (2015)
3. *Mindset: The New Psychology of Success* by Dr. Carol Dweck (2006)
4. *Atomic Habits: An Easy & Proven Way to Build Good Habits and Break Bad Ones* by James Clear (2018)
5. *The Third Door: The Wild Quest to Uncover How the World's Most Successful People Launched Their Careers* by Alex Banayan (2018)
6. *Secrets of the Millionaire Mind: Mastering the Inner Game of Wealth* by T. Harv Eker (2005)
7. *Grit: The Power of Passion and Perseverance* by Angela Duckworth (2016)

Learn How to Prospect

1. *The Seven Levels of Communication: Go from Relationships to Referrals* by Michael Maher (2010)
2. *Work by Referral: Live the Good Life! Proven Strategies for Success and Happiness in the Real Estate Business* by Brian Buffini and Joe Niego (2008)

3. *Fanatical Prospecting: The Ultimate Guide to Opening Sales Conversations and Filling the Pipeline by Leveraging Social Selling, Telephone, Email, Text, and Cold Calling* by Jeb Blount (2015)
4. *Rejection Proof: How I Beat Fear and Became Invincible Through 100 Days of Rejection* by Jia Jiang, Mike Chamberlain, et al. (2015)
5. *The Confidence Gap: A Guide to Overcoming Fear and Self-Doubt* by Russ Harris (2011)
6. *The 10X Rule: The Only Difference Between Success and Failure* by Grant Cardone (2011)

Build a Profitable Real Estate Business

1. *Brokers Who Dominate: 8 Traits of Top Producers* by Rod Santomassimo (2011)
2. *Ninja Selling: Subtle Skills. Big Results* by Larry Kendall (2017)
3. *6 Steps to 7 Figures: A Real Estate Professional's Guide to Building Wealth* by Pat Hiban (2011)
4. *The Book on Investing in Real Estate with No (and Low) Money Down: Creative Strategies for Investing in Real Estate Using Other People's Money* by Brandon Turner (2014)
5. *Giftology: The Art and Science of Using Gifts to Cut Through the Noise, Increase Referrals, and Strengthen Retention* by John Ruhlin, Drew Birdseye, et al. (2016)
6. *Purple Cow: Transform Your Business by Being Remarkable* by Seth Godin (2002)
7. *Raving Fans: A Revolutionary Approach to Customer Service* by Ken Blanchard and Sheldon Bowles (1993)

Leveraging Social Media

1. *The Conversion Code: Capture Internet Leads, Create Quality Appointments, Close More Sales* by Chris Smith (2016)
2. *#AskGaryVee: One Entrepreneur's Take on Leadership, Social Media, and Self-Awareness* by Gary Vaynerchuk (2016)
3. *The Road to Recognition: The A-to-Z Guide to Personal Branding for Accelerating Your Professional Success in the Age of Digital Media* by Seth Price and Barry Feldman (2017)

Social Situations, Negotiations, and Sales

1. *The Go-Giver: A Little Story About a Powerful Business Idea* by Bob Burg and John David Mann (2007)
2. *Go-Givers Sell More* by Bob Burg and John David Mann (2010)
3. *Never Eat Alone: And Other Secrets to Success, One Relationship at a Time* by Keith Ferrazzi (2005)
4. *How to Win Friends and Influence People* by Dale Carnegie (1936)
5. *Influence: The Psychology of Persuasion* by Robert Cialdini (1984)
6. *Never Split the Difference: Negotiating as If Your Life Depended on It* by Chris Voss (2016)
7. *Pitch Anything: An Innovative Method for Presenting, Persuading, and Winning the Deal* by Oren Klaff (2011)
8. *Captivate: The Science of Succeeding with People* by Vanessa Van Edwards (2017)
9. *Crucial Conversations: Tools for Talking When Stakes Are High* by Kerry Patterson, Joseph Grenny, et al. (2002)

Bonus Reads

1. *Rich Dad, Poor Dad* by Robert Kiyosaki (1997)
2. *The Compound Effect* by Darren Hardy (2010)
3. *The Slight Edge: Turning Simple Disciplines into Massive Success and Happiness* by Jeff Olson (2005)
4. *The Happiness Advantage: The Seven Principles of Positive Psychology That Fuel Success and Performance at Work* by Shawn Achor (2010)
5. *Daring Greatly: How the Courage to Be Vulnerable Transforms the Way We Live, Love, Parent, and Lead* by Brene Brown (2012)
6. *The Magic of Thinking Big* by David Schwartz (1959)

Add Your Book Ideas to the List

TIME-SAVING TASKS FOR YOUR ASSISTANT

Marketing Responsibilities:

For all new listings and any edits like price reductions, new photos, or changes in property descriptions, this is a sample checklist of marketing channels for you to use. The magic comes when you execute the checklist on every new listing, *every time*. This checklist is also helpful for removing listings once they are sold or leased.

1. Company (or franchise-provided) website for listings
2. Crexi
3. LoopNet
4. Brevitas
5. OfficeSpace
6. PropertyShark
7. Craigslist
8. Facebook (personal page and company page)
9. Facebook Marketplace
10. Instagram
11. LinkedIn
12. Brochure
13. Email marketing sent to all commercial real estate brokers (example: Mailchimp)
14. Personal website (example: nathanmatelich.com)
15. Property video (example: Animoto)

There are many other lesser-known commercial real estate websites that I post to or that are automatically syndicated via my franchise-provided website. I encourage you to create your own 30- to 40-point marketing checklist and ask your administrative assistant or marketing director to use it for every listing. Some of these websites and marketing channels must be updated or renewed monthly, and this is why I use a task-management software like Zoho Projects. The recurring marketing task reminders in Zoho Projects assigned to my assistant allow me to create a marketing system that produces truly epic results.

ADMINISTRATIVE RESPONSIBILITIES

Assistants can literally help you double or triple the amount of business you are currently doing. Get a task management system (such as Zoho Projects or Asana) and assign the following recurring tasks to your assistant.

1. **Check Marketing Websites Weekly:** Make sure they are all up to date and nothing will expire before it should.
2. **Update Clients Monthly via Email:** Create a monthly email update to each client by drafting a message in the broker's email and reminding the broker to either call the client or send the email.
3. **Weekly Listings Update:** Send a weekly email to the broker with all current listings, asking for any status updates – under contract, sold or leased, price reduction, etc. – to keep the marketing accurate.
4. **Check Listing Contract Expiration Dates Weekly:** Check contract expiration dates and give the broker two weeks' notice before any expirations.
5. **Schedule Social Media for the Week:** Create a plan for social media content for each day of the week, such as: Motivation Monday, Testimonial Tuesday, Listing Wednesday, News Thursday, Joke Friday, Property Video Saturday,

and Listing Website Link Sunday. Market updates and videos of the broker talking commercial real estate or success stories are always a hit. Schedule posts across Facebook, LinkedIn, Instagram, etc., every week using a software like Buffer, Hootsuite, or Zoho Social.

6. **Monthly Mailings:** Perform a data farm, have the broker write a compelling letter, and send it to a bulk mailing service.
7. **Ask for Client Reviews on Google, Facebook, or LinkedIn Monthly:** Create a draft email message for the broker to all clients who closed a deal within the last month, requesting they leave a review. Make sure to include links directly to Google (only if they have a Gmail address), Facebook, and LinkedIn so they can easily find where to leave a review. Use all reviews for Testimonial Tuesday social media posts, listing presentations and your website. Reviews and success stories are the #1 most powerful way to convince a potential client to do business with you.
8. **Monthly Email Marketing to Brokers:** Send emails monthly using Mailchimp (or a similar email service) to share your listings with all the commercial brokers in your area. If you have 30–50 listings, send the monthly emails broken up by property type such as office properties in January, retail properties in February, etc.
9. **Update Email Marketing List Monthly:** Add new contacts from your CRM to your email marketing platform.
10. **Quarterly Performance Review with Assistant:** The broker and their assistant should sit down quarterly to

discuss progress, difficulties, opportunities, and goals in a *mutual* performance review format. I always make sure to ask my assistant how I'm doing or what she needs from me to be successful. The best ideas on how to grow my business or improve our marketing often come from my assistant – so make sure to ask for input!

11. **Quarterly Email Newsletter to Past Clients:** Ask your assistant to come up with an email marketing template with the broker's input and ensure it goes out quarterly to keep clients informed about real estate market trends, to highlight new listings, or to share company success stories. I always fill mine with jokes, quotes, pictures of me with my family, favorite books I'm reading, and anything else that keeps people entertained or inspired to continue opening my newsletters. The goal is to communicate that you are a successful real estate broker who is relatable, down to earth, and shares common interests.
12. **Quarterly Email Marketing to Referral Partners:** Create and send a mass email to all bankers and referral partners with *all* your current listings to create credibility and show them the volume of commercial real estate you are moving. It also helps to keep you top of mind.

ACKNOWLEDGMENTS

This book is dedicated to my family and my mentors. All of the success I have enjoyed professionally is due to their support and mentorship.

First, I'd like to thank my amazing wife, Heidi Matelich, who makes me a better man. Not only does she help me stay grounded and focused on the most important parts of life, but she also does all the hard work at home raising five amazing kids. She is the best support system any man could ask for, and she graciously puts up with all my crazy real estate adventures.

My kids are young and don't know it yet, but they are some of the biggest contributors to my success. All the long hours and hard work are to leave a legacy they can be proud of and to create long-term, positive effects for many years. Everything I do is to create the best possible future for my family. It's also amazing how their "Have a good day, Dad!" comments as I walk out the door or big hugs after a long, hard day keep me going. I love you to the moon and back!

To my mom and dad, Craig and Mary Matelich, who taught me that Mateliches work hard and always shoot for the top. Because they always expected the best out of me, I continue to always expect the best out of myself. I'll never forget all the hours my mom invested in me on my road to earning my Eagle Scout or my dad putting in the hours to help me succeed in the classroom or on the court. My biggest job now is to pass on those same values and work ethics to my kids.

A big thank you goes out to my mentors. Steve Kenney was an amazing mentor when I first entered the business. He invested a tremendous amount of time in me and ensured that I had a rock-solid foundation to build on so I could handle any type of real estate transaction. I still remember our big "talk" six months into my commercial real estate career when he told me I needed to get more listings or I'd never make it. Four years later, I consistently had 40 listings, and I never looked back.

George Warmer has been the best supervising broker and managing partner I could ask for. He's the kind of guy who is passionate about ensuring that Coldwell Banker Commercial brokers are doing business the right way and holding ourselves to the highest standards. He's answered a million of my questions and never hesitates to help me get a deal done. Thank you for being a great business partner.

Blaine Poppler has helped me acquire and close more deals faster than anyone I know, purely from the fact that he has the textbook answer to just about any real estate question I can think of. I call him "Professor Blaine" because he never just gives me the answer to my real estate questions but instead takes the time to make sure I understand the why behind everything, which makes me a better broker. I love how invested Blaine is in my success.

David Mitchell is a stud who pushes me to sell more and become a better person daily. When he isn't dropping some serious real estate knowledge on me or doing deals with national retailers, he's comparing notes with me from great books each of us has recently finished. He's a phenomenal business partner, and his drive and work ethic inspire me to reach levels of success I previously didn't know were possible.

Lastly, I'd like to thank my assistant, Cindy Tapp, who is the "secret sauce" behind everything I do. Cindy keeps me organized, runs all my marketing systems flawlessly, holds me accountable, makes me look good, and puts up with my crazy ideas. She's basically like family and provides a level of support that any real estate broker would kill to have. And no, she's not available to help you execute all the great ideas and systems in this book because she's already too busy helping me!

ABOUT THE AUTHOR

Nathan Matelich grew up in Great Falls, Montana, and has spent most of his life taking advantage of the state's amazing outdoor activities – camping, boating, fly fishing, skiing, and everything in between.

To advance his education, Nathan moved to the Midwest, where he achieved a degree in Biochemistry from Loras College in Dubuque, Iowa, after which he relocated to Chicago for the next seven years to complete an MBA in Finance and Health Care Administration. While in Chicago, Nathan met his future wife, Heidi, who, ironically, was also from Montana. Nathan has had the opportunity to work for a Fortune 500 company, teach a master's-level business course, help an international electronic medical records company expand its sales and operations to the US, and become an energy efficiency specialist. He has invested in multi-family real estate since 2009. He was also able to help grow a utility cost reduction company's sales/operations footprint from one state to servicing all 50 states plus Canada.

When he isn't spending time with his wife and five children, Nathan stays involved in his local community by being active at his church and attending networking events to be a resource to other small-business owners. Nathan joined Coldwell Banker Commercial in 2015 after realizing his true passion is real estate.

Because Nathan does what he loves, he feels like he never has to "work" another day in his life.

In 2022, Nathan earned his Certified Commercial Investment Member (CCIM) designation. He prides himself on being an expert at listing retail, office, industrial, and multi-family properties and selling them faster and at a higher sales price.

Nathan attributes much of his success to his faith, church community, and Catholic roots. He has learned that God is the best business partner, and the more he gives back to his community and tithes a minimum of 10%, the more his business has grown. The greatest legacy Nathan plans to leave is through teaching his kids the importance of using God's gifts to help those in need and to make your community a better place.

"To whom much is given, much will be required."
– LUKE 12:48

Nathan Matelich
406-781-6889
nathan@cbcmontana.com
https://www.facebook.com/nathanmatelichrealestate/
https://www.linkedin.com/in/nathanmatelich/
https://www.instagram.com/nathanmatelich/

www.ingramcontent.com/pod-product-compliance
Lightning Source LLC
LaVergne TN
LVHW050825061126
851857LV00012B/983